The Man-You-All

The Man-You-All

A Guide To Save Black Women Time,
Money & Energy

J. Thurman

iUniverse, Inc.
New York Bloomington Shanghai

The Man-You-All
A Guide To Save Black Women Time, Money & Energy

iUniverse books may be ordered through booksellers or by contacting:

iUniverse
1663 Liberty Drive
Bloomington, IN 47403
www.iuniverse.com
1-800-Authors (1-800-288-4677)

Because of the dynamic nature of the Internet, any Web addresses or links contained in this book may have changed since publication and may no longer be valid.

The views expressed in this work are solely those of the author and do not necessarily reflect the views of the publisher, and the publisher hereby disclaims any responsibility for them.

ISBN: 978-0-595-49865-9 (pbk)
ISBN: 978-0-595-61282-6 (ebk)

Printed in the United States of America

To Tangela for helping me to regain my humanity.

J.T.

Contents

Part III

The Man-You-All is a concise source of reference for the sole purpose of empirically and emphatically dispelling the most prevalent misconceptions that black women have about black men.

(The Man-You-All will give real answers void of repercussions of socially unacceptable statements that if investigated, would provide an unbreakable paradigm for the masses. The Man-You-All does not discuss marriage, true love, or any get hitched quick schemes. The Man-You-All is a preventive strike against Nigga's and their bullshit.)

Liberate repress social construct

The Man-You-All deals with responsibility, sistas' responsibility and accountability for the shit that happens to them in their relationships. It is time to destroy the role of victim and take responsibility. Black men see the true power that black women have and how their laissez-faire attitudes about intimate relationships cripple their true potential and power over the "Black woman—Black man dynamic".

The Man-You-All talks about the brainwashing that takes place in young women's lives. The programming that molds and shapes not only gender roles, but also gender identity, simultaneously maiming internal constructs of self-reliance.

The Man-You-All discusses the myths that black women have about black men based on the immutable fact that black men are the villains and black women are the victims. The myths that black women have about black men are centered on plausible-deny-ability denial through *ignoring the facts*; undefined terms of engagement and fear to confront questionable situations. Also black women have a strong dependence on second hand information by scrupulous agents spewing the infamous "SUPPOSE TO", indictments.

Learn not to use pre-programmed responses that are predisposed for someone else's life to solve your problems. Instead utilize methods of self- introspection. Answers for your life are within, but few have the courage to go there.

The novice to the black man black woman dynamic would say communication (COMMUN-I-CATION)—is the key—HOWEVER—these people are full of shit. How can you commune sentiments that don't exist and never did with another person. What black women want to hear in crisis of an intimate relationship should be first inquired at the beginning of your first encounter with a potential suitor. Possibly, that person does not have the capability to deal with your needs. Find out first! Maybe that man does not have the capacity to express ideas, feelings and explanations you need to bring clarity to your mind.

The Man-You-All will answer some stigma's surrounding the "SEX" myths with true responses unpopular to those afflicted with the moral affinity.

The Man-You-All defines terms that are thrown around everyday in our smoke house conversation without knowing what they mean. The number of clichés that define our intimate relationships and our justification for our intimate relationship must be individualized and not left to outdated folkways and norms.

And last but not least, the Man-You-All will show black women how to save their money, time and energy. Simply, the best way to win the race is to go straight to the finish line or prepare in advance. There are preventive measures that can help you, small details that can make you Un-Fuck-Witable when you choose to deal with black men.

Let Us Begin!

I

The Brain-Washing
A
Fairytale for ALL

Once upon a time, a little black girl read a magical tale of a beautiful princess whose prince will come and give her undying love that would last forever. Horse shit! First, how does the prince know that she even exists? Second, why does she wait for a man to come and save her? Third, why does she need undying love from a stranger? Why can't she possess this undying love from within? All of the days, weeks, months and years that have passed, she never chose to look within to find a deeper love nor did she look within to define specifically what and how she needs to be loved. Fuck that, he would do that for her and after the newness fades she will blame him for not providing what she needed.

In a land far—far away lived a beautiful maiden forced into indentured servitude to her evil stepmother and three evil stepsisters. (Stop, all the women are evil and distrusting, jealous and out to steal a man). She wishes for a chance to rise above her circumstances and dreams of a better life. Enter a fair godmother who hooks her up to out stunt all the other women. The coupe de' grace is that the Prince chooses her and takes her from rages to riches. Happily ever after, the end!

First, the effect of the evil woman who plotted and schemed to take her love interest is an important point and is an example of distrust being taught among women early. Black women distrust other black women to the point they won't even have them as friends nor bring them around their potential love interest, period. Dissension and scheming among black women can never be productive, KNOCK THAT SHIT OFF!

Secondly, the fair maiden never leaves her shitty situation but rather waits for magic to save her. Thirdly, without hesitation, the handsome Prince delivers her from evil and punishes her wicked antagonist. "Take that BITCH!" He hands over a kingdom on a whim because she is "Fine." Poppycock!

*(Fairy tales breed unjustifiable excuses and create a slothfulness that gives them the belief of entitlement without effort or merit.)

With black women, the brain washing begins early and often. Fairy tales exude racist blatancies, self-identity issues, and misplaced concepts of gender roles that fossilize how she perceives her role inside the "black woman-black man dynamic".

Black women utilize the fairy tale concept of engagement with black men. They speak in terms of "chivalry" but do not have a clue as to what chivalry is. Chivalry is one of the components to the fairytale conspiracy and an idea that black women have added on to it everyday.

The knight in shining armor throws down the gauntlet in defense of a woman's honor and was slain by the dark knight. Black women think this is love, devotion and romantic. No, it is sadistic to ultimately seek a form of satisfaction in the fact that someone died for you in this way.

Fairy tales are the primary way children form beliefs about themselves, relationships and love. Fairy tales are also a black woman's first look at

What's chivalry?

gender roles and gender identity. Fairy tales often provide a visual and emotional medium that last a lifetime in reference to what love is and how love is obtained. These images that have imbrued the black woman's mind rather it be through the digital medium or orally recited every night are the black woman's first concepts and principles on how and what black men are "SUPPOSE TO DO". Right there is the example on how black men are, "SUPPOSE TO" act regardless of the way black women treat black men. Mothers and fathers actions in their relationship are too inconsistent but Cinderella and The Prince's relationship are constant and dependable every time that little girl presses play. The Hunter saves Red Riding Hood and the Prince risks his life and limbs to protect and save the day.

Every woman likes a little crazy in her man.

Fairy tales create the need for dependency and often breed a recapitulated scenario of helplessness—rescue—salvation and deliverance from evil. However, the evil threat also seduces (Hint: Why black women love Thugs). The allure and seductive qualities of the wolf, for example, in Little Red Riding Hood; the Beast in Beauty and the Beast suggest a deeper truth.

Black women are told that they are to watch out for the wolf for just as in Little Red Riding Hood, he possesses major seductive qualities. These qualities are lust, mystery, adventure, (an intoxicating opiate like effect), violence and enchantment. She wants to be seduced and her fear upon first contact intensifies the wanting. She wants to be taken! This only explains why Little Red Riding Hood disobeys her mother's explicit instructions and strays off the path. She also engages in flirtatious conversation with a wolf while simultaneously giving him precise directions to get to her grand mother's house. Little Red Riding Hood is seduced by a charming, clever, entity who is most effective because of the taboo's that she was not "SUPPOSE TO" follow. The color red, which is the color of her hood, is also the color of love, passion, violence and lust, which all are to a degree madly seductive. She will not part with her red hood, which is her security because she feels exposed without it. In Perrault's original version, The Little Red Kap, Little Red Riding Hood gets into bed naked with the wolf without her red hood exposed. She then blames the wolf for the shame she feels after being "EATEN". But then the hunter crashes in and redeems her virtue.

The Problem is CHOICE.

Black woman resort back to fairy tale morals and values confused or confronted with their own self-perception. They avoid being sexual creatures to affront the moral affinity. Black women are good girls, not good women. Black women pose as one who is pure and innocent; pristine and untainted, as is the state of the pre-pubescent girls, which fairy tales almost exclusively defer to. These women are victimized by their sexuality and Man-ipulated by the authoritative women in their stories. These women never mature physically therefore they never mature mentally into womanhood.

Most need a "WOLF" to give them an outlet to take responsibility over their incumbent sexual and sensual development. (Myth—"A real man knows what to do without me telling him.") Without the wolf's(BIG TEETH-to devour the flesh; BIG EYES-to hypnotize; BIG FEET-dick myth; BIG ARMS-to embrace; BIG LEGS-to harness the body; plus a dash of fear, danger and excitement without it a black woman is not truly seduced). The Hunter, even though he saves Little Red Riding Hood, can't wet her panties, period. The Beauty and the Beast scenario is one of the most deadly and classical cases of—"When fairy tales go wrong". Studies show that girls enamored of fairy tales are more likely to be submissive adults and by extension, more likely to experience violence in romantic relationships. (Go Google violence and fairytales) the study was performed by University of Derby Master student Susan Darker—Smith in a piece called "The Tales We Tell Our Children".

Honestly, black women often make bad choices when picking mates to begin a <u>companion based encounter</u> because of the Beauty & The Beast theory. Black woman believe that if they up hold their holy trinity of HOPING, WISHING, and LOVE, coming from the fairy tale gospel that their life will be happily ever after. Black women believe that if they can alter their behavior to cater to what he wants, he will turn into Prince Charming. (Hint: YOU CANNOT CHANGE A GROWN ASS MAN, PERIOD. STOP THAT BULLLSHIT!) Change your eating habits, change your hair; change your dependence on a man—hell, change your number. Black women want that fairy tale wedding and give up and go to Jamaica. If given a choice, they would take Cinderella's wedding but a dream deferred is like a raisin in the sun. Even when adult black women are referred to as princesses, they shine with nostalgia more so than if you would call them a queen. (Nobody wants to be the Queen because she has to rule and respond to the needs of many and she is worshiped as such. In contrast, a princess is a ruler in waiting and has no responsibilities other than preparation in stasis for a moment she puts off as long as possible, adulthood.)

Stop Waiting for Him!

It is pathetic. He sees these tendencies you have developed and either thinks you are hopeful or loathsome, the perfect prey for the wolf. Women go out and line up on the wall, looking flawless from head to toe, for a non-existent being to come along and be the "ONE". His ass ain't coming and in the process a multitude of good brothers pass these women by in defeat of the black woman's' fairytale complex.

Black women surround their early ideas of love and relationships around the fairy tale complex and some never progress beyond it. The formula of hope, wish and love equal to a person who disillusion themselves just enough to get by. During all the time it took for her hair to grow, Rapunzel never devised a plot to escape. Her grand locks grew long enough for some man to climb up the tower to save her. Why would she not just use her hair as a rope and climb down? I guess that shit would have been too easy. The Frog Prince gives us still another valuable moral lesson. A Princess comes across a frog that was enchanted by a spiteful fairy. The princess comes to like and then love the frog enough to kiss him, which changes the frog into a handsome Prince. Should the princess have asked more important questions before kissing the frog? Why did the spiteful fairy enchant or turn the Prince into a frog? Was it because he was already an ugly frog on the inside and she just matched the outside with the inside? If that is the case, what makes the princess think he would change? Once a frog, always a frog. <u>That Nigga' will never change, he will just suppress his true nature just long enough to pacify your misplaced wanting for hope, wish and love</u>. Every woman thinks she is the one to change—that man—but the truth is no woman is that special.

The point is that Fairy tales, when not uprooted with experience and social maturity, distort reality for Black woman who deal with black men in relationships. When black women meet attractive black men whimsical thoughts of love at first sight and Prince Charming flash across the movie screen of life with expectation of living happily ever after. And when there is work to be done black people get divorced. The problem is choice. How can black woman avoid the, "Fairy Tale Nightmare"?

Define relationship and then re-define it according to your individual specifications. Divest from the notion of "wait and he will come", and stop compounding this cliché by mixing in misinterpreted religious proverbs with, "God will provide a good man for me". God has a boundless universe to consider and will not be responsible for your fear, ignoring the facts and bad decisions. Faith without works is dead faith. Get to work and work your way back to the Goddess, not the princess that you are. Create a goddess like aura and he will worship you. The fairy tale develops a good girl prototype based off purity innocence and naïveté. Black women draw off this prototype to mask their devilish seductive qualities or they use it as an excuse to why they do not know how to suck dick. Every black woman mature socially in the arena of relationships differently and many stop in their teenage years. Those who do not involve inward more than they evolve outward use the good girl prototype to mask their ineptness to mature into a woman and make the appropriated adjustments.

Tolerance and Tendency

It is the general conscience that a majority of heterosexual men's motives, methods of acquiring means and identity is centralized around one thing, the black women. A black mans status, clothes; location of residence, vocation and every key component is compartmentalized around, "Getting a woman". Now a chump ass Nigga' would participate in the conscious lie that he disagrees-but lets look at the inscrutable facts.

Every woman "needs" a project to give her a purpose, position and place in the "relationship" and then she knows better. Some women do not understand that all projects come to an end, then what.

The society we exist in emphasizes family with no clear road map on how to accomplish this feat. Black culture pushes the words manhood with no lucid paradigm on what the term means. Throughout this Man-You-ALL, we together will investigate the infamous "SUPPOSE TO" theory, which binds a man to an unwritten code of conduct. This code of conduct is primordial based on the archaic code of chivalry which we will briefly discuss.

The folklore of the black man's credo has morphed from the post civil rights manifestations of God, family and community into money, hoes and clothes. Throughout the history of the blacks in this country, family preservation has always been primary and other goals and aspirations second. The man is the head, the hunter-gather for the wife and child first. Black men are "SUPPOSE TO" provide for the wife and then to-get-her they produce offspring. But how do we arrive at the finished product?

It starts with the "Chase" to attract a certain black woman. Contrary to the black woman's belief, every black man's preference and taste are not individu-

8

ally catered to him and he will not settle for anything less. So ladies, if you are not the right height with the right complexion, he will find that type whether it come hell or hot water; he will get her because being satisfied and complaisant will not due.

(Hint: Why do men cheat?)

To allure the black woman, the man only needs three key elements:

1. The illusion of respect, universal gestures of pseudo chivalry.

2. The illusion of riches, e.g. appearance, car etc....

3. The illusion of independence.

In a group situation, the addendum to the 3rd element is the "Co-sign" by her companions.

The choices that men make to accrue the three key elements to allure black women are universal and go back to the old adage, "A woman don't want a man who ain't got shit". With this in mind, black men must adapt with technology, fashion and status recreating identity under the guise of pressure, promise and pussy. Some men live for the "Chase" more than the perpetual price at the end. Black men become consumed in the "Chase" and lose focus on what it is they are trying to accomplish in the first place. Black men also lose focus when black women settle for the deliverance of vanity, no substance, and large feet. And it is at that point where the lines between family and fucking cross, and then blur. Whose responsibility is it to get it back on track?

Everything black men do is based on the black woman's approval. The model, color and year of your car; the color style and fit of the clothes you wear; the level of education; earning potential; the value of the property where you live all play factors in the black man's quest for acquiring the key ingredient, the black woman. The black woman is essential for the longevity and lineage of a black man's preservation of family.

With this in mind, let's look at what black women do not know about the control within the black woman-black man dynamic and how their tolerance or tendencies direct the beginning, middle and end of the "Chase". The black woman does not know that she controls every unconscious decision the black man makes involving the "Chase". The black woman maneuvers and guides unbeknownst to her. If black women knew of the influence that they have over black men their decisions and choices in dealing with black men on every level would be drastically altered fo' ev-va.

With this new insight a matter of "Tolerance" must come into question. For every problem that the black woman has with the black man, she has yet to establish that because of her tolerance for bullshit and other deviate trifles is in ownership of her dilemma. If the general conscience is that black men are guided by the thoughts and opinions of black women in their quest to fuck, freak, finesse or family them, then why do black women tolerate mental and physical abuse so freely. The most popular answer among my contemporaries is that self-esteem issues serve as the reason for sadistic—masochistic rela-tionships. The self-esteem theory is convenient to those who want to wrap themselves in the same smug self-righteous indignation that they read about in a book.

What is self-esteem?
And how can you individualize it so that it has
Meaning for you?
Self-esteem—1. To hold one self in high regard; respect.

All in all that's cute, however, the truth is a black woman will subject herself to anything when faced with the reality of being alone. The true and living tes-timony is seen in the mirror of the black woman who suffers this truth every-day or someone you know who is beyond saving. A black woman will suffer through insurmountable shit to avoid being ALONE. The idea of being alone is the black woman's greatest fear and greatest weakness.

Black women—pay attention—to the details on how subtle your powers exist and how it can grow.
If the black woman does not like the style of shoe a brother wears, he will change it. If she does not like the cut of his hair, he will cultivate it, and so on. So what makes a black woman think that she has no effect on the attitudes and philosophies, which ultimately alter the action of black men? It is not a matter of a black man saying "I do it to get the pussy"—he still does it—and whatever he needs to tell his boys or him self in the mirror is strictly personal and irrel-evant. The age and videos in the mass media have shown us just how transpar-ent men and their motives are. Black women do not have to fall victim!

Black women tolerate what they do based on the lie that "If I love him he will change", or fool themselves into thinking it was just sex and of course the oldie but goody, "I think that Nigga' got some money". They open themselves up for a world of hurt. But somehow it's never their fault. If the <u>dick is good</u>, addictive characteristics turn into obsessive tendencies, which mask the one truth that is hidden in a labyrinth of fallacies of clichés. People who share any dangerous addictive personalities all have similar traits, repression, denial and misdirected anger. When faced with nothing (NO-Thing) or no one to occupy their time space and life, beyond friends and family, black woman need objects to fill the void and black men <u>become</u> that object.

Black women tolerate pure insanity for the sake of not being "alone". They marry down—low brothers, black men who can't manage any relationship and dealings with their child's mother. They tolerate a lazy bastard, literally, eating all the Toasted Oats while watching ESPN eight hours straight while <u>black woman</u> toil and work to keep the cable on and gas in a car he cannot fill up after emptying. What the fuck! Black women tolerate black men fucking their friends, sisters, cousins and who ever drops it like it's hot, for what? Cause you don't want to be "ALONE".

Masochistic: (maz-o-chis tik) Abnormal sexual excitement marked by pleasure in being subjected to physical pain or abuse. 2 Derivation pleasure from being dominated mistreated.
Sadistic: (se-dis-tik) A sexual perversion in which gratification is obtained by inflicting physical and mental pain on others.

Black women use the moral affinity clause to justify enabling the black man with their acts of lunacy, visa vie love. Black women enable before they are evaluated to assess where there deficiencies lie. Being over whelmed by the newness dilutes ones logic and reason, necessary tools and one of the first steps to saving the black woman time, money & energy.
1. Quiz that Nigga—all good prospects need a thorough exam, find out how he can benefit you for whatever services you need at the immediate time.
2. Check his intelligence and sensitivity levels with a joke at his expense—see how he thinks on his feet.
3. Avoid clichés in initial conversation, e.g. how old, what school, children etc. These clichés only waste time and never get to what you really want to find out and if you disagree you have an even worse problem.

4. Ask him to qualify statements, e.g. you are beautiful. Blow up his trick and ask him what makes you so beautiful specifically. That question alone, in the first part of the conversation, can eliminate eighty percent of your problems.

These mechanisms are the first and last line of defense against your—SELF. The "SELF", that uses hope and attraction to make life altering decisions.

Black women enable black men from being responsible, and they foster their inadequacies under the moral affinity of being a "Good Woman". The black woman's tolerance hides her own inability to make good decisions about dealing with black men. Tolerance leads to tendencies that perpetuate a life cycle of how black women do or do not properly take control of their choices. Instead they just blame their scapegoat, black men. There is no true in-depth thought process to distinguish what the black woman pretends to want as opposed to what she needs. The black woman never stops to first clarify within herself what she needs specifically. The act of performing a self-inventory in all aspects of life can prevent incidents in dealing with the opposite sex. Women spew incessant clichés that have no individual meaning to them and the evidence is always seen in the result of every bad encounter with the opposite sex. Black women say they want a "real man", and for him to treat her well, specifically, what does that mean to her. Few sit down and even hash out the details so their wants are specifically catered to them. Some people have no imagination and seek to live the wants and desires of their friends because they are to apathetic to be original. And if she is specific then why does she continue to communicate or even deal with a man who is incapable of complying with her specific wants and needs. The problem is choice. Why does a black woman continue to ignore the clear signs of a disastrous situation before hand?

(Because she has no strategy!)

Black women surrender their divinity and dignity for a piece of <u>dick.</u> Then the question asked quite to infrequently is "Is the dick worth it", and the answers are "yes". "Is the dick worth destroying my credit, severing my family ties, ruining my career and true friendships", and the response is, "hell yeah".

Tolerance—4. Physiological resistance to poison

Tolerance of destructive and demonstrative acts lead to tendencies that are used to further exacerbate a weak ass situation. Once a man knows how to manipulate the twist and turns of your desperate need to not be alone, prepare for the ride. People have a fear of being alone, however, because of the crippling repressive state that black women have been subjugated to this fear phobia has intensified itself and the proof is in the state of the black man-black woman dynamic. One would say that it is the individual's choice to tolerate or put up with certain behaviors and I would agree. Unfortunately, the problem is choice. Who is responsible for the choices one makes? Black women deflect responsibility and blame the villainous black man because it is convenient and because, "men just want some ass and that's it". Black men (pacify) in order to (gratify), these are their most important tools of manipulation. Someone might add that there are many reasons why black women do what they do and that every woman is different. Cute response but if the black woman did not tolerate being treated like a refuge by the black man—IT WOULD NOT HAPPEN.

The black woman's power is vast and infinite and if she will not learn to harness it the white woman will.
Side notes:

1. Black women coddle and pamper too soon in attempts to appease (deceive) usually to compensate for their lack of depth as a person or their desperate need to fill the "VOID".

2. Black women throw pearls to swine and blame the pig for not appreciating the gesture. When a person creates self-inflicting disappointment by way of expectations serve as enemy in most encounters. A good man is right there, but your choice to pick the asshole falls in line with the tendencies of your masochistic inertness.

3. Some black women make important decisions all day in their careers and make and/or save corporate enterprise millions of dollars and leave the responsibility of companionship to fall in the hands of some one who does not have a clue. The most sacred of palaces should not be administered by an imbecile. Prevent your emotional demise.

The Moral Affinity

What is the moral affinity?
The moral affinity is a code of procrastination, morals and defense mechanisms black women use to justify why "Nigga's ain't shit".

The key component to the moral affinity is perception. Those who use the moral affinity are oblivious to sexuality desire and mortal frailties. This is reinforced with the "Good Girl "idiom complimented with the "Good Women" clause. The moral affinity is void of the individual's personal truth and is saturated with outdated forms of virtues, archaic mores and gender role constructs. The moral affinity's premise is based on the reality that black men are the "villain" and black women are the "victims" in an unfair, unequal social and moral construct. Therefore, black women have created their own infallible system of checks and balances. This system of checks and balances are founded on the one truth that every black woman knows "I don't owe that Nigga Shit".

Another stone in the foundation that erects the moral affinity is a conditional folklore that makes black women feel that black men are obligated to surrender his sovereignty, hopes and ambitions to her every whim. This delusion of obligation that black women create for black men in a form of indentured servitude to black women. No, black men just <u>pacify</u> in order to <u>gratify</u>. Some black women co-habitat the black man's obligation to black women with the infamous <u>"SUPPOSE TO"</u> law. Men are <u>"SUPPOSE TO"</u> provide every pleasure, need and want for the black women. Black men are "SUPPOSE TO" do all these things in spite of the black woman inadequacies in public, in private and in the bedroom. How dare some black women with their no dick sucking, no back rubbing, no consideration having and no glass of water getting asses, how dare you request the boundless universe and the entire world's bounty. Nigga Please!

14

Black men are "<u>SUPPOSE TO</u>" do all things in spite of the black woman's incapability to boil water or sew a button. And as the old faithful phrasing of "do it yourself", pours out of the mouth later tonight, she will squeeze her hands or electric device between her legs and say "I don't know why I can't find someone".

The moral affinity is a code of predisposed prejudices against black men, which is the basis of the myth that black women have about black men. Black women hide behind the moral affinity to mask the terrible decisions they make with black men. Black women play ethical and moral dress-up but never search and find answers and means to practically fill the roles they pretend to play. <u>Self-proclaimed ladies,</u> without the knowledge of how to become true ladies, model themselves after those who secretly hate and denigrate them. Keep your originality and authenticity.

(Hint: Why black women hate other black woman)

The moral affinity puts black women above sexual desires. Black men are the only beings that ever want sex because the moral affinity releases black women from natural innate involuntary sexual desires. The moral affinity allows black woman to judge other black women who own their sensuality and sexuality. Primal ignorance of sexuality is some of the residual remains that accompany the moral affinity. However, to avoid the disappointment of human contact with black men there is an endless supply of size C and D batteries to help remain steady to the discipline of the Moral Affinity.

There is a preset grouping of reasons why "the black man ain't shit" and the moral affinity preaches them all, therefore, I need not list them. A black woman carries with her a prepackaged brand of charges against the black man for she is the protector of "The Virtue and The Good". The virtue she guards is the virtue of hypocrisy and cowardice. The good she preserves is the good of self-righteous indignation rooted in the—Holier Than Thou-method of assigning blame and fault.

Fact—Being a "Good Woman" does not make you a good woman.
Fact—Hiding behind "The Good Woman" clause does not excuse the fact that you make terrible decisions in choosing men.
Fact—Choosing a white man or choosing another woman does not change your poor judgment—ONLY YOU CAN. So look at your decision-making or literally look in the mirror either way, take responsibility.

The problem is a choice not chance.

Cultural pathways make the level of excuses some black women use vast and too ambiguous to fathom. Non-secular belief gives The Moral Affinity an additional dimension. A faith-based component gives it validity and an air of divinity and purpose.

However,
Fact—God helps those who get off their asses and make appropriate changes to make better decisions about their choice of a companion.
Question—Have you helped yourself realistically?

Fact—<u>That</u> neither devil nor god is responsible for your decisions which, sometimes, were made with the skill and tact of a truck stop whore.
Question—How much thought did you alone put into your thought process on your approach and method of attraction?

Fact—God is not a matchmaker, pimp, or Madame.
Question—Have you thought sincerely about a more cost effective way to search for possible companions instead of expensive cruises and other find love quick schemes?

Some black women think they are better than the sum of their parts. But nature straighten-s them out every time. You cannot run from your body, mind, and spirit.

Fact—God is not a postman who delivers good men, who if, most black women had a good man, would not know what to do with them if they had one fall into their lap, to your door.
Question—Are you cautious in being specific for that good Man, who maybe more man than you can realistically handle? Do you really know what kind of man you can handle from what you know about who you are?

Fact—If you leave it up to God you will be alone, period. If a good man comes along, it was not solely God alone, it was you letting go of your ego and receiving what opportunity God has presented.
Question—How capable are you to manifest changes in your life based off how well you know yourself?

Fact—God will help you gain the knowledge you lack in different aspects of your approach when encountering black men, AS YOU DO THE WORK TO CHANGE.

Question—Are you willing to do the work or will your girlfriend do the work for you? Or will a book do the work or will your fear of not getting hurt, do the work again with the same results?

The moral affinity assists black women in avoiding deep introspections that fuel the engine of denial, avoidance and immutability. Black women, who use the moral affinity, use it unconsciously (Assignment: Google defense mechanisms and learn more about them). It permeates through their soul and bleeds out their every mood. The moral affinity is consistent in delivering a message that is chaste and upstanding void of immorality and indigent character. It resonates a spiritual yet somewhat religious undertone masking sexual frustration and/or inadequacies. This is why the relapse of <u>addick-tion</u> and going to church occurs so often.

—Most black women would not be at church if they had a man—

(UNDERCOVER — OVERCOVER — BATHROOM — BATHHOUSE — CLOSET — LIVING ROOM — BACKSEAT — CARPORT — GARAGE — MILE HIGH CLUB — STORAGE ROOM — ALLEY — ELEVATOR — TRUCK BEDLINER — PARK — WHIRL POOL — MOTORCYCLE, IN THE TRUNK FREAK!)

The moral affinity's purpose is primarily establishing the fact that the black woman is not a WHORE. A black woman would rather be set on fire than perceived as a whore. The Moral Affinity protects against this indictment and anything that resembles it.

Being a bigger person, being a better person is this a credo of people that use the moral affinity? Black women who use these particular accents are the best example of people who squander unnecessary amounts of money, time and energy trying to prove how moral and just they are. These black women are targets to be robbed and pillaged by manipulative cock's men. Listen, your mental and physical health is at risk and everything you have worked for.

This is not the time to do the right thing.

- Child support

- Debt accruement

- Theft

- Abuse

Black men abscond free and clear because the black woman let them walk
<u>HOPING</u> that they will do the right thing. Sometime people who do wrong
to other people get a way with it for a whole lifetime and receive no retribution.
And if you see punishment happen to them, do not think it was your crime
being vindicated, it usually was some one else time for vengeance. Among your
peers, you explain how it is the right thing to do, but in the quiet reflection of
your solitude you know you have been fucked.

The problem is <u>Choice.</u>

Do you choose to take a preventive measure or fall victim to your nobility and
good sense of morality? Hold that nigga' accountable or Shut UP! If the reward
of being screwed over is just being right and moral, then that is weak. Black
women breed laziness by permitting a questionable situation to go unchecked.
Black women traditionally yield their authority to plicate the black men's street
corner created sense of manhood. It is easy for the encounter → meeting →
relationship → to be controlled by black men because that's what black men
are <u>"SUPPOSE TO DO"</u>. It is easier to relinquish responsibility and decision
making to the black man because responding to a problem within any form of
relationship is work, period. The moral affinity allows the black woman to run
from hassles like intelligent participation and preventive assessment because
when "IT" blows up, she is still the victim and the black man is the villain.

The "IT" that blows up is the sweet beast that is called the unspecified, undefined and ambiguous social association. The moral affinity allows the black
woman to excuse her poor choices in dealing with black men and elevate her
above reproach and fault.

• Can the black woman specify what she wants without the fear of running
  the black man off? Let that buster go, please!

• Can the black woman define what she wants without worrying about the
  disillusionment of perception or judgments?

• Can the black woman directly communicate the term of her position in her
  encounter with black men without using the phrase "you know what I
  mean"?

The moral affinity stereotypes, assumes, defensively presumes, cultivates cliché
axioms, fingerprints, blames, castigates and condemns all to guard against the

entrapment of disappointment when dealing with black men. But everything has its flaws and small points of vulnerability.

1. Lust—Black women get horny.

2. Loneliness—Innately want company of opposite sex—same sex—be real, universal laws apply.

When these two reach critical breakdown, bad decisions are made—with the Wrong Nigga' Again.

The Good Girl idiom and moniker represent virtue, decency and purity, which are good in practicality, but like a white wedding dress the meaning behind it, is just for show.
The moral affinity exists because black women never mature the Good Girl model into the Good Woman paradigm. The Good woman paradigm is more polished and more chiseled in the arena of specifying and defining her place in the black woman-black man dynamic.

The Good woman does not allow fear and fate to maneuver her relationships with black men; she stands to the courage of her convictions and is accountable.
Black women who use the moral affinity simply do not know what the hell they are doing with a man and blame black men cause to them truth is "Nigga's ain't shit".

The Precept

W hat if you could stop that Nigga's bullshit before it happens?

"Changing the past"

Do you ever wish you could change the past? If you could change the past,
you would
Be able to correct every mistake, avoid every accident, and never experience
the pain of regret.
In fact, you can very easily change the past. You simply must do it before the
past becomes the past. This very moment where you are right now will soon
be in the past. So now is your golden opportunity to assure that it will be a
past you'll be pleased to have.
With care and focus with love, discipline and positive intention, you can do
just that. You can change what will soon be the past into the best it can be.
Imagine not having to wonder what would have happened if only you had
been a little more careful, thoughtful or diligent. Imagine living your life with
no regrets.
Imagine it, and know that right now is your chance to make so. Use this
moment to give yourself a past that won't need any changes at all.
—Ralph Marston

What if you could prevent disastrous life changing events before they happen
and leave his ass at the bus stop where you found him?
Women who give power to the unpredictability of life negate their own influence and power to take charge of not only the out come but also the size and
shape of their own situation before hand. The Precept cuts to the chase and
intercepts the bullshit before its six-month's later to the day you wish you never
met that sorry ass nigga'. In theory the Man-You-All is designed to stop black
women before they choose black men with their pussy instead of their heads.

20

(Hint: Usually the first question women ask a man is the most unimportant)

This is not a game, your time money & energy cannot be taken back, returned or swapped out for another purchase item nor can it be given back to you in exchange for credit on your account. In theory, the Man-You-All is designed to stop black women and keep them from consistently making the same faux pa's when meeting someone either by chance or calculated spontaneity. The Precept is the science of logical selection that defeats the lazy tendencies to "just let things happen". Just letting things happen causes humans more grief than anything.

The game is not to game with the basic principle of engagement but to clearly define what you can deal with.

• What do you want and how do you want it?

Women must know what they want from any encounter that occurs. These are things that need to be thought out first before the throbbing of your clitoris takes over. The Precept is a concept that states that truth is individualized and only revealed to the woman who uses it. Application of any truth is one form of a working reality with self and kind.

(Reality—if you want a man, do not waste time with any other misdirection or meandering around what you want. The game's women play, though fun, and end up confusing not just the dumb ass listening to it but also the proprietor of said bullshit.)

The friend to lover scenario is horse shit. This kind of fool proof thinking only works in a world of make believe. Men have enough friends. Women need to be something different. This requires imagination and paying attention to the mans needs. Men want your pussy primarily and your resources secondarily, period. Take control! Do you want the dick or the promenade that is convincing him that you are not a whore? You can burn his plans of deceit and treachery by owning your sexuality and not running from your pussy. It is not morals or discipline you're installing at that moment of confrontation with temptation; it is fear of the fact that the bare essence of you is out of control and you are ill equipped to deal with it. Let him know up front with no hesitation or fear and remove expectation with a real working situation. Or you could wait until you're slashing his tires and ask why couldn't he love you, because you started off with "he's just a friend", that's why. If he is just a sex buddy is real first, CAN YOU HANDLE IT. The truth is that very few black women can handle it.

(Hint: Stop justifying your motives or action. Men don't care how virtuous or whatever cliché black woman spew. Perception does not matter when it is time to have sex.)

The black women must come clean and decide who she is. ARE YOU A:

1. <u>JUST A SEX PARTNER</u>

2. <u>SERIAL MONOGAMIST</u>

3. <u>RELATIONSHIP WOMAN</u>

4. <u>MARRIAGE WOMAN</u>

Only you can reveal these things to yourselves. The basic principle of a companion-based encounter is to treat every meeting, no matter how incidental, with respect and importance. Because those that do not show reverence for the situation, six months later deserve what they get, a heaping flaming bag of shit. When you leave important self-defining issues open for ambiguous interpretation, you will not be happy with the result. The problem is choice. Who are you when it comes to dealing with black men?

Just a sex partner—this type is rare because of the discipline and isolation of "SUPPOSE TO" in contrast of who she is and the liberation sex provides. Black women never learn to out grow the MINE STAGE. <u>Black women believe that there's only one DICK and that DICK is theirs</u>. MINE—MINE—MINE is sprawled out and their childish greed cripples their sexual maturation. Women who conquer the mine phase have healthier sexual experiences and are more in tune with mind over matter. The just a sex partner reaches a nirvana of deep intro-personal perfection and is closer to conquering the tools of deceit that men use because she can mirror his apparent abandonment for restrictive sexual codes of conduct.

The Serial Monogamist—has one rule. I can only fuck one man at a time. This because the moral affinity disassociates from any resemblance to whoredom. The Serial Monogamist is bound by "The Rule" because she alone will uphold the morals and decency that a lady is "SUPPOSE TO" exhibit.

(Hint: The same people and religious bodies who create codes of ethics and morals about <u>sex</u> never follow them and are the most sexual deviant people on the face of the earth. Why do you think people go to church to find a freak?

The best freaks sit near the preacher, I promise. They are not hypocrites. They just fall in line with natural frailties, but they fall harder because they try to work against innate probated sexual progressions.)

Serial monogamist follow a second parameter, they only stay in a relationship with a person, man/woman, for six to eight months and then continuously repeat the cycle. The reason is their fear of commitment, disappointment and the fact that they will be exposed as a fraud as a human. Remember, perception plays an important part as well because the way the black woman looks aesthetically is the only thing that matters. "I'm in a relationship with one person although I already have the next five lined up". Family and friends judge because it looked good on paper; when the body (man) is gone it always ends up, it was the man's fault. Who can question or bring inquiry to a dead corpse? And isn't it the woman side that really matters after all is said and done. In its totality, black men might as well wear a T-shirt that reads "I DID IT", because his side of the story has no side, front, back or foundation.

Black men don't get intimate with their woman because they don't trust her. The only thing they can trust is the fact that most women will betray their trust and throw intimate thoughts and actions in their face without fail.

The Serial Monogamist justifies their actions to fuck and pleasure themselves under the invisible cloak or monogamy and all other aspects of a relationship become meaningless clichés that she uses, cycle after cycle.

Relationship woman—these women need a relationship to complete the Afro—American dream that black men adopted but took back to the orphanage. She must now carry on because of new financial prosperity and new gender role reversal, Black women feel that if a black man enters their sacred place, not their mind but their pussy, they are in a relationship, period. There is nothing to discuss or question.

What is a relationship?

Relationship—connection, a significant connection or similarity between two or more things, and the state of being related to something else. 2. Connections in regard to how people behave and feel toward each other and communicate or cooperate.

The Relationship Woman cares nothing about a comprehensive and thought out romantic or intimate relationship nor does she know the difference. She just wants the pseudo structure of a relationship. The Relationship Woman cares about the relationship device which is: man → woman→ dating→claiming→commitment→my boyfriend, my man →letting it just happen → doubt → insecurities →break up→ sex partners →next in line.

The Marriage Woman—is a dual dichotomy of reality and unreality. She is the obsessive control freak that has done nothing but plot for her moment from the first time she saw Cinderella. The other side of the coin is the aging debutante that has looked in the mirror and sees her beauty dissipate with every moment and must marry the next good person that comes along. For the sake of youth, let's first deal with the topic at hand.

Some black women from an early age, dream of a fantastic wondrous wedding and that's it, period. The groom (man) is window dressing and mostly filler and bound to live out the rest of his days in a constant cycle of performing cliché husbandry duties with no other logic than he is "SUPPOSE TO", the endemic response for all of his questions.
There is no between—black man meets black woman—they are together— marriage done deal. The ceremony is all that matters. The ring is all that matters, (platinum & karats, BITCHES baguettes and weight HOES.) The perception of empty love with no substance is all that matters. Who has time to know yourself much less somebody else? You can work on that after the honeymoon to Dubai?

Then there is the aging beauty that has burned through her twenties with the speed of a highly flammable device. She still is a young boy's fantasy and a married woman's nightmare. She is still stunning and vibrant, but dislikes what she sees in the mirror. She has come to a point of quiet desperation that is unspoken, even unto her closest friends, although over the years close friends have had no place in her lifestyle. She has only had her beauty and her smarts to guide her. Suddenly, one day she goes out and cannot get that drink as fast as that twenty-one year old temptress can and then the bottom falls out. Her method and reasoning for getting married is strictly for security reasons. The aging beauty is more tolerant than a younger fawn; she is calculated and never deceived by the illusion of love over food, clothing and shelter. She knows her victim well and is very careful in her selection. A "so-called" woman would ask her secret and learn from her for she has many experiences that an average looking women does not know. Her victim is forty to middle age possibly and once a good looking man, graying or balding who is in desperate need of re-definition and aesthetic filigree. He is insecure and she does not care if he cheats; her concern is home base and the knowing that he feels absolutely lost and destitute without her.

The Marriage Woman is a fictitious victim of her own devices. The Marriage Woman never matures as a complete being and along the way there are too many pieces scattered over a lifetime. There are too many gaps of ten year relationships and four year affairs trying to get to the ceremony. Wasted opportunities to teach about the real "YOU", which if obtained can feel the void created by disillusion, fear and undefined individualized mores and irrelevant false standards. Save your time, money and energy for in this scenario there is no take back.

The Biggest Lie Ever Told

The biggest lie ever told is of course, "I Love U". However, for the direct purposes of The Man-You-All I have chosen another. The biggest lie ever told encompasses two key components that appeal to the black woman hypocritical ethics and anti-whoredom campaign. These two key components are built on the foundation of bullshit, displacement of guilt and reverse false concern. The key components are respect and time.

"I can only respect a woman who makes me wait before we have Sex"

This is the only lie that men actually tell one another when a woman is not around. Let's break it apart piece by piece: 1—I can't respect a woman—first things first, either you respect women or you don't, it is a basic qualifier of humanity. Men use black women's talent for judging other black women to make this lie sound more believable. While divesting her from the other "whores", he can place her in a place of honor and nobility. Like warm sweet oil being poured into the black woman's ear hole, she begins to soften her defenses and perception about this black man who spews this propaganda so skillfully. Some black men don't respect black women period. It is the black man's job to isolate the black woman into a cone of silence where all she sees and hears is he and this makes the lie more obtainable and effective.

Listen to the first part of the statement again—I can't respect a woman; this means he can only respect a woman with conditions and limitations with provisional clauses. This logic brings to mind that his LOVE must be the same way and there can be no unconditional LOVE and to a black woman unconditional love is everything, period. Men utilize this rhetoric to inform the average woman they have a standard (separate and unique). That they are not phenotypic and shallow and their standards appear moral and introspective into the being of the whole woman—DAWG DUNG. Respect is. Respect is not earned in every situation especially dealing with the black woman-black man dynamic. Modes of time restrict it.

How do black men earn the respect of black women?

You either respect black women or you don't, there is no in between! The next time a black man disgorges the word respect, ask him to define it and then think why he can't supply such basic alienable rights to all black women. (Hint: This is how you smoke his punk ass out.) If he says I only respect women if they respect themselves he does not know what respect is and can not respect you. Don't waste your time, money and energy trying to correct him. That woman he can't respect probably is in dire need of some unconditional respect, first.

Respect:
Attitude of admiration
Thoughtfulness
Consideration
Regards
Polite pleasant feeling
Not to go against; violate

The second part of the statement 2—"who does not make me wait", implies men are patient, for one, and two, this gives women a feeling of being special, LIES, LIES, LIES I say! If you need expensive Cuban cigar smoke blown up your ass, COOL. A man, who allows a woman to think he will wait for you to re-virginate yourself and only you for his next sexual experience, successfully is a genius and a pure craftsman. (And those women who tell their girl that she told her prospective beau to go ahead and fuck someone else does not mean it and just does not want to be considered insecure (punk) in front of her girl). A man who waits freezes a black woman's judgments and simple logic by making such statements. "He must be fucking someone else". Yes, he is fucking some-one else. He is fucking the woman who doesn't fall for the lie and is loyal to her needs. He is fucking the predecessor who came before you whose waiting time is over. A cool rotation of three is great and very manageable.

How much time do you need to respect someone?

If you met a great figure in history on a plane and talked to them the whole time about life and interchangeable experiences, is that enough time to respect someone? Respect is void, in lieu of the fact, a sexual encounter may ensue. In the case scenario we are speaking time is your enemy. Time allows doubt, fear, insecurities and unfounded prejudice to creep in and destroy an uninhibited attitude that is free from judgments and expectation. Time also deludes the black woman into thinking about concepts of next time, next week: next month the future and my favorite, FOREVER.

What time can do for you!

Time gives black women a gauge to see if this brother is for real.
Time permits black women to recall the fairytale construct that ends in happily ever after.
Time grants black women a chance to build up the anticipation of the next moment, next call: next kiss next vile deprivation of any authentic connection.
Time makes black men want the experience more vehemently-but not sincerely.

The cruelest injustice is when a woman makes a man wait for a sexual experience and it turns out to be putrid. A true sexual experience worth waiting for stimulates all his senses not just his crotch.

(Hint: The only reason black men don't call black women back.)

But when the time comes all some black women have to offer is rhythm-less hips and the pornicopia of a three position slow motion grind. In all of the time you made him wait, what were you doing to make this "Special Moment", unique and different Yoga, Pilate's, maybe a belly dancing class. If time materializes respect then maybe time corrects sexual deficiencies or magically gives a woman the flexibility and imagination to warrant a call back, maybe.

The lie worst of all and most importantly play off the black women's fear of being perceived as a "HOE". If money is not exchanged up front before a sexual act you are not a "HOE". A "Hoe" and "Whore" are different all together and identifying which one is which can save you time, money and energy.
If you:

• Ask, "What can you do for me", before starting any conversation upon first meeting a man.

• Repeat over and over, "I can't stand a broke brother".

(Hint: Black men can't stand a broke ass woman-with weak head)

- Knows hoe terminology verbatim.

- Must receive a trip, car note, rent, and mortgage payment etc … before sexual favors especially if you use the words "sexual favors".

- Wears a hoes uniform for the purposes of soliciting patrons.

- Ask how much money you got before you say, "hello".

- Only deals with older men using the words "more stable" as justification.

Then you might need to pursue the craft or perfect your craft on white men—Thank God for white men. The one thing that all black women run from is the one thing they hope to be. Black women repress their sexuality from their own enjoyment and somehow offer it for sell. They sell it so that they feel that they are not being <u>USED</u>. A preemptive strike to defuse the inevitable fact that you emotionally are out of control when penetrated well, firmly and deep can save you money, time and energy. Stop running from the invasive truth and take control. Even a whore cums and enjoys it, so what does that make you.

II

Myth #1
Why do all black men lie?

Convenient Truth: Simple, Black Men lie to avoid inevitable confrontation that black men are ill equipped to handle intellectually.

Actual Truth: Black men lie because they are not held ACCOUNTABLE. Patterns of behavior grow over time and are strengthened only by the woman's avoidance of said behavior being expressed upon and reinforced.
Black men lie because they can utilize the need that black women have for fantasy. A fantasy based off assumption and a craving for an alternate reality.

Black men lie because black women allow them to. Black men know that at that very moment, when the lie is spoken, she has no other choice but to accept it. Soon, after each time the women receives the lie, she builds up a tolerance to the lie. Then the EGO kicks in and retaliation barges in and replaces the clarity of the mind with the classic game show called, "I caught that Nigga lying again", which is followed by the spin off, "Pay Back Is A Bitch". The prize is stupidity and the justifiable answer to all the questions is love.

Keys to a Good Lie:

• Speak with conviction. (plant the seed of doubt)

• Maintain good eye contact. (never stare)

• Validate points of your lie with thoughts, words and phrases the person you are telling the lie to uses and conclude by saying, "You remember don't you".

- Keep the lie short and plausible. Never go outside of your own character too far to be believed.

Keys to being lied to:

1. Deny all logical intuition.(2nd guess yourself)

2. Ignore the facts.

3. Have faith instead of evidence.

4. Worry about what you can not control.

5. Be a control freak or continue the existence of such behavior. (allow insecurities to guide you)

6. Trying to catch somebody in a lie …

7. Concern yourself with the illusion of not being loved.

8. Imaging being alone, again.

Black men lie because it is a perverse thrill and danger in getting caught often to evoke a misdirected sense of passion out of the black woman. Lying also helps black men to mask a truth that would threaten their pussy, (lifestyle) comfortable situation and allowance. Black men bring into play a woman's first sense of reality pretend or their addiction to fantasy.

Myth # 2
All (Black) Men Cheat!

Convenient Truth: Black men cheat because the women that they are engaged with at the time have no clue how to captivate his audience and release her selfishness long enough to surround him with his passions. She does not know how to find out what these passions are that he has. Nor does she have the patience to provide him with these passions that are deep in the recesses of his heart. So, he moves on endlessly questing to find the benefactor of his unfulfilled dreams, his personal Dream Merchant. (Hint: Passion does not mean fucking)

Variety is not just the spice of life. It is a cold-blooded reality for both men and women.

Actual Truth: The deeper question is to be specific and accuse black men of cheating with what and with whom. Brilliant pseudo philosophy tells black woman that black men cheat everyday but not just with another man or woman, but with food, PS3's (PLAYSTATION 3's) sports, pornography, work, money, Internet etc … Cheating has re-defined itself with the help of insecure black women who think that if the black man removes his eyesight, thoughts or attention from the black woman for a second, he is delinquent in his duties as a man and is therefore cheating.

- A black man is cheating when—he confides in someone else besides the person he is having sex with.

- A black man is cheating when—he breaks the rules of the game to gain an advantage over the manipulative psychology of the woman he is having sex with.

35

Point blank, black men are cheating if their actions, mannerisms, tone and postures do not mesh with the exact sentiment and pre-programmed mental diet the woman he is having sex with has prescribed.

Yes, all black men cheat according to the new definition, but all men do not commit acts of infidelity. Infidelity requires marriage 1st, then a verbal declaration between two or more people in an exclusive sexual relationship. Black woman and black men don't sit down and discuss the terms involved in their encounter with one another. Their dealing in term of dating + sex = the assumption of a monogamist relationship. When black men penetrate black women sexually they are in a relationship—<u>GAME OVER</u>. There is nothing to review or interpret. If there is no verbal declaration there is no act of infidelity. Men know this and women ignore it.

Black men and black women, all depending of their individual level of attractiveness and confidence, are constantly looking for the best option. With black men it's cheating in the most cliché of terms. With some black women they simply are browsing the market looking for the most viable business acquisition by consolidating and merging her potential assets and the new, marks capital ventures. The black woman cheating is pure pimping wrongly accused of HO'ing and misinterpreted as gold digging. Some black woman pimp by the book while others waste gourds of time, money and energy. The black man's cheating is usually clumsy, maladroit, and tactless and most of the time performed with the ware with all of a nine-year-old boy.

Remember: when you ponder the question of cheating and/or infidelity, know that asking the right questions can save you great amounts of time, money and energy.

Ask Yourself:
• Are you an asset or liability?
• What do I possess to secure his or her loyalty?
• How well have I mastered The Three P's?
1. Pussy
2. Passion
3. Personality

Remember: You choose to empty yourself into another human being recklessly, using the grand cliché of them all, love as your justification.

You think you can will or control the actions of another by HOPING, WISHING & PRAYING when you simply cannot.

The problem is <u>Choice</u>.

Are you a victim of the villainous black man who manipulates your "Love"?
Are you still a nine-year-old damsel in distress or can you save yourself?
Can you infinitely save yourself, time, money & energy by not worrying about things you cannot control?

Myth # 3
Black Men Do not Communicate!

Convenient Truth: No, black woman waste time with men who are incompatibly incapable of communicating to their much specified set of comprehensive sensory mechanisms.

Actual Truth: In the beginning, there was no reason to think that having a man who is unable to express himself so that you can overstand the message being given is important, until they have to respond and cannot. Black women pride themselves in their ability to be (smarter) and more (intelligent) expressive than black men and consistently trying to "Catch" them in an act of malfeasance. Question, do black women want a companion who is unable to express him or her to foster a superiority complex? If not, then why waste time with someone who is not going to give you the type of communication that fits your personal needs. You cannot turn a tiger into a dog just ask Siegfried & Roy.

Do you know what your personal needs are as far as communication is concerned? If so, list four right now on this page.
Exercise:

1. _____

2. _____

3. _____

4. _____

Most commonly black women would say that communication is something that you have to work on because it takes time to develop. Generically that comment goes into the cliché box as do most convenient excuses for avoidance not dealing with their own ideas of communication. Most black woman think that every time a black man is at a loss for words that he is lying or caught and his silence is not just an admission of guilt but a victory for her insecurities. This is just not the case. Every black man is not a wordsmith. Black woman "ASSUME" that an adult-sized man is "SUPPOSE TO" know how to express himself and make adjustments to cater to the woman he is dealing with.

Not Realistic

Exercise: Ask a black woman how long should she wait before she make a decision that there is no chance for an effective means of communicating between her and the person that she is dealing with. Note: The response that will lead to more excuses that feed into the addictive chemistries that form in the brain. We get addicted to excuses that ultimately send chemicals to certain portions of our brain that provide a calming balanced state.

Find out if you have a communication problem before:

• you have get married

• you have a child

• you really need it

• you commit acts of loyalty and chastity

• you get emotionally involved

• you waste more money, time and energy

There are ways to find out in the initial conversation whether or not "THE POTENTIAL" has what you need. The author does not prescribe an interrogation but investigators, lawyers and other law enforcement officials get paid to know how to ask the right question. WARNING—Do not takes the human element out of the engagement but do not take it for granted either, remember it's not a game! Here is some T.I.P.S.

1. Avoid the normal question (E.g. how old, where are you from, school etc....)

(Usually the first question a woman ask is the most insignificant)

Once men hear these cliché's, which most women think are important questions but are not, they begin to metaphorically dig into that ass and the game is afoot.

For those who say, "who has the time", certainly makes time for hair appointments and make-up than make time for the rest of the body, which holds up the head.

2. Choose a topic of interest to talk about and let him talk he will often dig his own grave. See if he gives you an opportunity to dialogue, a man who does and does not over talk you is key.

(Men don't realize that if they are attracted by a woman they often time fuck it up by talking too much and saying too much. Listen for the lyrics to an R&B song, if he sounds like one excuse your self immediately.)

3. Listen with your ears and not your crotch.

4. Look him in the eyes.

Everybody plays the part, however, either you have a good skill set for communication with a particular person or you do not, you cannot fake it. That particular black man who you cannot communicate with you will find someone to relate with. It just isn't you.

Stop Wasting Your Time, Money & Energy
Your attachment with HOPE, WISH and LOVE cripple your development into a whole being
FOCUS!

For those who overstand the importance of spotting good communication and bad communication know what I'm saying, and for those who do not need to ask and prepare for the inevitable

The problem is <u>Choice</u>.

Myth # 4
It's hard to get a black man to commit!

Convenient Truth: No, it is easy to get a black man to commit to a worthwhile cause but it is damn near impossible to get any black man to commit to crisis unless he has a superhero complex.

Actual Truth: Black women, ask yourself, are you a crisis or a worthwhile cause? Do you want someone to fund your every whim and wish? Are you an asset or a liability? Do you hinder or enhance the men or women lives you've spent time in? Was it for profit or pleasure? Are you enjoyable to be around or are you just tolerable to be around until he cums?
Now if you're a good woman and do everything a black man can dream of— Stop—you should not because it breeds dependence, comfort and a state of being complaisant.

> Find a Happy Median.
> Do not be his Mother!

YOU CANNOT GOOD WOMAN YOUR MAN INTO A COMMITMENT, PERIOD!
He will or he won't, if you don't talk it out beforehand, the shit gets deep.

Define: What a commitment is to you, say it out loud and ask for a verbal definition from the person you are having sex with. If you wait for the black man to give you what you want or anybody for that matter, you are a fool, period.

Exercise #2: Define what a commitment is to you?
(Write it out, the visual of actual words helps you more than you would think.
Take the time to know before it is too late.)

    If you are with someone or going to be with someone who makes you afraid
of rejection <u>LEAVE IMMEDIATLEY</u>!

    If you are with someone, who won't commit, based off him knowing that
you have verbally declared that you want a commitment, <u>LEAVE
IMMEDIATLEY</u>!

The longer you wait it out, the more time, money and energy you are wasting.
If he or she comes and tries to lure your pussy back with an expired commitment, it is like spoiled milk; it is no good to consume and nourishes nothing.
Anything at this stage is not sincere nor is it long lasting. An authentic and
sincere gesture is not based on fear of somebody else getting "my pussy" or an
ultimatum.

The problem is <u>Choice</u>!
Stop wasting your time, money and energy.
You could have fucked his boy hassle free.

Myth #5
Black men don't take care
of their children!

Convenient Truth: Of course some black men take care of their children. The black woman that argue to the contrary delude with their ideas about fatherhood that all return back to this one fact "that nigga' ain't with me/or marry me he ain't shit.

Absolute Truth: The core of the matter is not if the black man's check is on time to help maintain food, clothing and shelter but if the relationship between the black woman and black man is maintained.

Myth: The money the black man pays for child support is just for the child's food, clothing and shelter with every woman.

• If you have moderate transportation, I understand.

• If your baby's mama is using child support or sometime vengeance payments for a Lexus, Mercedes Benz, or BMW payment, no one understands.

What about the other children in the house whose father, sperm donor, biological etc … do not pay child support? Is that check for that one child going directly to him or her?
No, the money the black man gives, if any, is never enough. Food, clothing and shelter are never enough. Teaching life skills, life lessons, providing guidance at a child's beckoning call is just enough. The intangible gifts of devotion, loyalty

and humanity are also key footnotes in child rearing. But, did he have those attributes before you let him between your legs?

The brass tacks of it all, where the entire rage, anger and betrayal lie, is in the fact that, "he does not take care of me". Regardless of the unanimous deliberation of guilt that black men face-one truth supersedes the issues of abandonment of his duties as a father—his duties to provide for the black woman first. The child is a tool of control and manipulation. In an attempt to preserve all the attention, some black women would never have children because it takes the attention away from them. Then, there are black women who have children because of the opposite effect it has on men. Black women feel that if they have a child by a black man, it ties them into the vine. The vine of financial support stability—emotionally and physically. For all of the broke Nigga's this applies but in a situation where a black woman's love is given pure and recklessly. Some black women feel that all they have to give is their bodies and a child is an extension of their mind, spirit and body. Any hint of rejection of the child is first a rejection of their love and then their worth as a being. Vengeance is a dish best served cold. For those black men who supply their monthly vengeance payment but sacrifice the requested quality time per request of the black woman, I understand.

Reasons:

1. You do not want that nigger around YOUR child.

2. You do not want that bitch that nigger is fucking around YOUR child.

3. He is just a terrible influence and you disagree with how he lives his lifestyle. (The same lifestyle that attracted you to him)

4. He contradicts what you are teaching your child by undermining your authority.

5. He does not do what I say.

6. He betrayed me.

7. He did not marry me instead!

8. That's my ring, that bitch is wearing!

Bitter maybe! However, for those that get along with their baby daddy, sperm donor, DNA sponsor etc … I applaud you. Even though every chance the black man gets he's trying to GET BACK—either in the pussy or in the comfortable confines of your DOJO. If he can give you the illusion of a make shift family to get you off his ass he will. Black women use the excuse, "he is the father of my child"—to justify—fucking your baby daddy. The truth is you did not want to be alone and you just wanted the dick. You do not need justification to please yourself, ever. A child becomes the pawn of manipulation and control that the black woman use to control the black man with. Black women do think that "baby makes glue". Using your children to exploit your involvement is done for the following:

1. She can't make ends meet.

2. Sadistically but true, "I like to see him jump through hoops".

3. I don't want to be alone in raising a child.

4. He will come around in his own due time and embrace me 1st and my child 2nd.

5. That's my dick!

The point is simple condoms break when misused. Oral or dermal contraception may have side effects or not be 100%. But making dumb ass choices will get you pregnant by a man, who in the first place is incapable of being a father and in the second case inept about being a good person. I'm not saying look for a good father type instead of a great lay, I mean who has got the FUCKING time. If you go raw that diamond dick should come with insurance if stolen. Blaming someone and calling someone an imbecile for not taking care of his or her own children is common, but not as uncommon as common sense.

The problem is <u>Choice</u>.

What could you have done before hand to prevent this? If you do not know or want to seek solutions that you do not have, your problem is bigger than <u>Choice</u>.

Myth #6
Black men get a GOOD WOMAN and don't know how to treat her!

Convenient truth: Black men don't know how to treat a "GOOD WOMAN" because they are ignorant (ignore—ant—1. Lacking or displaying a lack of education or knowledge 2. Not aware: uninformed) of the methods and techniques that are required to treat themselves much less another person well. Some black men barely know how to treat themselves and any attempt to extend outward to another person is truly stretching out more than the individual can handle. And quite frankly, some men never think about it to be honest.

Absolute Truth: Who says that a self proclaimed "GOOD WOMAN" is authentically a "GOOD WOMAN". Black men perceive, a "GOOD WOMAN" in a way that is individualized and personalized to them. Black women do not ask what a good woman is to the person who they are engaged with because that makes them seem like a novice. Black woman are "SUPPOSE TO" know what black men want and need innately. This statement is ludicrous and absurd.

First, ask someone you are potentially interested in what is a good woman. If he cannot give you an answer, don't expect him to receive what you have to give, as you think it should be received. If what he wants is not in your repertoire don't start reaching or try to over compensate; be creative in what you have. If his list is too long don't deal with him. If his mama comes up in his description excuse yourself because there is someone else waiting more realistic at the other end of the bar.

A black man will know a "GOOD WOMAN" because she matches his perceptions as to what he sees as a "GOOD WOMAN". A good woman is an individualized fit not a force fit. A black woman could cook, clean, wash her man's rims, suck his dick while he is watching the Super Bowl with a bowl of nachos balanced perfectly on her head, but that does not make her a good woman for him. Forcing their own brand of "GOOD WOMANISM" the same way with every person that they are dating or sleeping with is selfish and foolish, but when it blows up in their face they need someone to blame. It serves their ego and moral affinity and no one else.

In answering the question
Why is it that black men get a good woman and do not know how to treat her? It is simple, he is just not equipped with the means (emotionally and mentally) to do so and for women who see glimmers of hope, I say the dick was just good enough to delude yourself. Your wishing and hoping will not make him appreciate you the way you think you need to be appreciated.
Stop spending money on a person when it does not mean any thing to them—all because <u>YOU</u> think that's what a good woman would do!
Stop wasting energy on a person who is oblivious to your efforts because it does not apply to them!
And stop wasting your time trying to invent new ways to waste your money and energy!

The problem is <u>Choice</u>.

Myth #7
Black Men Change after Sex!

Convenient Truth: No, Black men don't change after sex they bend themselves to the anticipated mood of the moment that follows.

Absolute truth: Black men wait in limbo trying to feel out the black woman's lead. Will she be cool? Will she get possessive? Will she blow up my phone? Will she stalk me? Does this mean that we are in a relationship? Both male and female responses are initially based off one condition and that is the quality of the booty. Black women and black men ponder the same question about post-sexual trauma. However, black men are left with the brunt of the backlash primarily coming from black women and their issues with sexual insecurities and their performance. NO ONE TALKS ABOUT SEX BEFOREHAND. SEX JUST HAPPENS. I don't mean placating the real issue about sex with, "I'm going to tear that pussy up, or my favorite" I'm gonna fuck the shit out of you. I mean talking about real subtext that matters. Do you enjoy sex? Do you only have sex to satisfy the other person out of guilt or obligation? Are you possessive? Can you separate sex from fantasy love? Does sex mean ownership? Are you a sexual person? Do you participate in exploratory sex? What is acceptable and what is not acceptable in sexual play? Do you perform oral sex? Are you open to other people in sexual play?

Not talking about sex after or before and "just letting it happen" excuses you from the responsibilities of the aftereffects.

Avoiding people who don't talk about sex or are ashamed of the subject is a definite time saver.

48

Black men follow the lead of sexual situations if the right woman is in control. If a black woman has not defined her sexual identity she will have problems. If she worries about the changing or the behavior of another person modifying she will have problems. If she worries about how many women a man has slept with she will show weakness and expose the fact that she is a sexual novice. Never show your hand. Men and women are who they are before they met each other. There is no deception perpetrated on either party only the deception that your own mind plays on it self when it is time to see people as they really are. You had a hunch that something was wrong, but fuck him or her anyway. Men and women try to appease the other by giving to one another a glimpse into a world of unreality that does not last more than five seconds after the orgasm or six months into the affair. The only change black women do not have an issue with is when "the change" falls in their favor by chance. Black women can guide the outcome to their favor where the only <u>chance</u> is the <u>chance</u> that they create. Black women can mold and shape the outcome if she is smart, tactful and in charge of her sexuality.

Helpful Hints:

- Find out what you like first.

- Fuck him. (A real woman knows what I mean and if you don't know ask one.)

- Get yours with every muscle, nerve, curve and contour in your body.

- Find out what sexuality is and the difference between sensuality.

- Explore your body. Go Tantric!

- Stop worrying about the "what ifs" (They create more problems than they are worth).

- If he gets attached or nutty have an evacuation plan (The old passive aggressive of "he'll get the hint" to avoid confrontation shit is obsolete.)

- Do not have sex because someone else wants it, that shit is so junior high.

- Sexually gifts are not bargaining chips for an emotional debt.

Exercise

Define Terms:

1. Sexuality, Sensuality

Many will say he just wanted the pussy but the real truth is "she" just wanted the dick and sometimes something else to follow suit. Black women do not admit aloud, that sometimes it's just about the dick, out of fear castigation in the arena or public opinion. Black men absorb a lot of the guilt in a sexual encounter because black men always want sex; black men are nasty perverse beings; black men are sexually more primal than black women, supposedly. When in actuality, black women are the ones that are sexually ravenous but cannot express it or won't express it out of shame. Black men change, however black women change as well, but to displace the changes that take place in them they mandate that it's the black men who shifts since naturally black men are the villain and negotiators of lascivious behavior.

In truth, black men do not change, only the environment changes; the place where the sexual act morphs and subsides. Black women create a mental environment to give the act of sex life and once this environment is corrupted with doubt, fear and guilt the black man is the scapegoat. Black men accept it because if the sex is great from her perspective she will be back repeating the same cycle over and over.

The Real
"He wasn't like that at first."
Yes, he was but your variant dependence on hope and "just letting things happen" instead of having a plan got you blindsided.

"He used to be different."
No, he is the same person; you're just not horny now.

"He never did that before."
Yes he did, you just never saw him physically do it.

"You can't know what someone is going to do"
True, however you can pay attention instead of trusting your desperate sense of denial which leads you to take unnecessary acts against what you know is right.

Simply, if the sex is bad, black men leave sometime right away. Sometimes after a series of sexual debaucheries, but they leave. If the sex is great, black women know and it is left up to them to control the outcome and vice versus. Lay clear defined lines down, get Ice Cold in your delivery but definitely have a plan. Don't let your situation handle you with compromising and mediation. This is a defining moment not just for the right now but for a better understanding of you regaining your identity. When done properly, no man will give you problems you don't want.

Black women who worry about why black men change after sex can never make a separation of the physical act from the immature expectations and hyperbolized fantasies of grandeur created. Usually, they go straight for a relationship model using the old bait and switch paradigm instinctually out of habit. Because we depend on our own set grouping of personality traits to guide us through any encounter based on engagement, we think that's all we need and we are always wrong. Because who sits down before to think realistically what comes after sex. The change that happens after sex whether negative or positive is a crapshoot best left to gamblers and fools, not to adults who are responsible for their mental and physical well-being.

Stop worrying about things you can't control.
Stop creating expectations about how someone is "SUPPOSE TO"
act after sex.
Find time to figure out how "you are suppose" to act throughout your life.

The problem is <u>Choice.</u>

Myth #8
Black Men Are Not Responsible!

Convenient Truth: To the short and the sweet of it, it is what it is. Black women's pussy dominates them in ways they are ashamed to think much less say and choosing a responsible man is not on their primary agenda until she reaches thirty-five.

Responsible—Accountable
To take action independently
Being the cause of something
In charge of something
Reliable
Financially sound

Absolute Truth: Black women only care about a black man being responsible when a child is involved. Too late! When the sex is reckless and perverse, who gives a flying fallacio if he can count much less be responsible and pick you up on time. Black men and their veneer of irresponsibility exist because they are given duties and responsibilities that they cannot get done and then blamed for their ineptitude. If a black man chooses not to be responsible, you do not need to waste your time, money and energy. If he cannot respond because he does not have the method nor the knowledge on how to be responsible. Do not waste your time, money and energy!. Responsibility is learned and not genetic. If your man's primary caretaker did not teach the <u>man you are having sex with</u> responsibility you sure as hell cannot. To assume otherwise is dangerous. To

Irresponsible men are reckless, and do not over think THINGS. They are more exciting and dangerous.

Responsible men are lame, PREDICTABLE & boring.

assume and use naïve statements such as "SUPPOSE TO" leave a margin of interpretation that has fueled the fire of prejudice and stereotyping.

People claim that all people in general, know and were shown how to be responsible, false. We see the signs all the time and not just about a person being irresponsible but in every way people disappoint us and we ignore it because we tend to see people as a reflection of ourselves and disregard the truth. We live on the principle that all people are good and live in a good responsible way but they all do not. The only way to see people as they are is to divest your sense of morality and ethics and master self-introspection that allows you to cut through the BULLSHIT.

A father or mother showing children how to perform a responsible act doesn't mean that they're showing them the practical application of such said act. Therefore, it means nothing (E.g. mathematics, cleaning a room, paying bills), period. If you think those opposites attract and if you're not the responsible one then he must be, think again. Such a mind state could cause the child you conceive over a bottle of Grey Goose or Hennessey many problems.

The problem is <u>Choice.</u>

You don't have to be bothered with a slew of character flaws if you do not want to. But pay attention to the details.

Myth #9
Why Do Black Men Play So Many Mind Games?

Convenient Truth: Black men play mind games simply to distract black women from the real issues at hand.

Absolute Truth: The key to any great illusion is misdirection and slight of hand. Basically, the black man's job is to get you looking in one direction distracting you with "Relationship", while he fucks with your time, money and energy all in the same breath.

Focus

When a black man has nothing to offer of substance, he gives the black woman "Relationship". Relationship is a kit that enhances his personality, looks and credit to a certain level. And the secret weapon in the "Relationship KIT" is the mind game.

Focus

Every woman likes a little crazy in her man. And the crazier the man, the better AND exciting the challenge.

Black women fall victim to the lights, camera and spectacle of not the person they are dealing with, but their own E.G.O (Exercising Genius Obnoxiously). Black women are the most intelligent beings between the two genders and those that know are aware, that intelligent people are the easiest to "Man-ipulate".

Focus

Black men use the mind game to compensate for things they don't know about women. Mind games are a tool of control when a man goes through his personal inventory and realizes he does not have anything else to offer to keep that woman he's dealing with attached. But you need good dick and dramatics to starve the mundane and hydrate the dearth of the everyday.

At a young age, black men learn mind games trying to out wit their mothers or female primary care takers. Testing the limits of unconditional love is the occupation of a young black boy's life. The charms that black men learn if any, is tested on his mother. If honed and utilized properly, it is his gateway to a life of privilege and frivolity. Black women want to feel honored and loved. Manipulating these things that they have been deprived of is essential for mind games to work. If black men can learn *"The thirstier a person is the less likely hood is that he will look in the cup before he drinks"*. to manipulate their mothers to get what they want then next on their list of things to do are your time, money & energy. If you are a black woman who craves and desires an extra dose of dramatics and excitement, it is real easy to substitute a relationship of substance and replace it with a wonderland for the black woman to exercise her insecurities. When this happens, black men have free reign to drain you dry of your dignity, time, money & energy.

Focus

- Know what you want.

- Know why you wish to be involved in any and every situation with men.

- Know how to get it and when.

    Usually black men depend on black women innate instinct to react to start the mind game.

Be Cool!

Most black women do not know how to engage in conversation or effective dialogue, so the mind game is a tool to see where your interest lie and how far you will go.

(Hint: Learn to initiate conversation and take control of the verbal dialogue; this helps women in situations where they are overwhelmed by a man who is very attractive to them. But don't talk too much, the key is to listen but remain subtly dominate.)

The mind game can only be successful if you are a reactionary individual (emotional x 10).

Most people watching a great magic trick think about how it is pulled off and for two minutes they are just in awe. Other people who watch a good magic act automatically try to figure out all of the angles and will never figure it out. Then there are some people who enjoy the skill and craft of the illusion, get entertained and never think twice about it. These people are immune to the mind game and black women should be too.

The problem is <u>Choice.</u>

Myth #10
Black men will fuck any thing that moves!

Convenient Truth: Black men are more promiscuous and black women are less sexual and more selective with chosen partners. Black men prefer quantity to quality, but black women pay more attention (to someone who will not make them feel sexually inadequate because of their own lack of sexual experience). Black women believe that love limits judgement in the sack) to qualitative attributes.

Absolute Truth: The more you fuck the better you get at it, if you are willing to grow and perfect skills. A lousy lay is always a reason to leave your ass. Ignorance is no excuse for the law. Black women who make this statement are referring to a privilege that black man "so-call" have to exercise their sexual liberties at will regardless of the consequences and societal repercussions.

The honest justification behind this myth is black women feel that any women, other than themselves, are a subspecies. Black women feel that the "ANYTHING" is immoral, cheap looking, tawdry and lacks basic human decency and possibly a better fuck than they are.

The Jealousy Clause serves as the true manufacture of this myth. There are two reasons why this myth exists.

1. She is disgusted with her cowardice.

2. She fails to see, "why not her".

Most women are disgusted with their dearth of courage and their inability to respond to not just the everyday wants and needs but their own introspective dichotomy much less dealing with a man. Most black women admire the women they scorn and socially castigate in secret. They want the courage to leave that bullshit relationship; bullshit fuck buddy, bullshit job etc … They admire the stripper (Shoe model) on stage that not only liberates her sexuality but also uses it to make slaves out of both men and women alike. The woman that calls or title "ANYTHING" is free and does not need her female friends to co-sign for her in social situations. She does while you and your fears calculate.

What does she have that I don't have?
A go get it attitude that has eluded you.
What attracted HIM to a woman like that?
Matters of attraction can be as unique as fingerprints themselves.
What secret does she have?
Simple, she does what you don't do, will not do, or know how to do and even more so are not willing to do.

Some black women never stop playing dress up. They dress up their dolls; their friends, their parents; the truth and they dress up men with the type of women they want to be but are afraid to become. They also dress up men with women who compliment them externally. For women who think black men are the only ones who can fuck anything and get away with it you are making excuses and feeding your fear. Those who use the Moral Affinity, then re-virginate and masturbate, to avoid human contact physically and mentally is weak and pathetic, pay them no mind. Those who say black men will fuck anything that moves have never been fucked or are too afraid to fuck because the line is longer for those who wait.

The disclaimer here is not whoredom or promiscuity; it is about judgement and freedom from it. Those who do not live in the moment, "Choose" not to act out the moment. The unconscious mind delays the any reaction until the moment is gone. Liberation comes from within and perception and judgement are tools of envious bitches' either male or female.

Some black men might fuck anything or is it that they won't fuck you. The "Choice" is simple. To be fucked or let your girl get it.

The Choice is inevitably <u>Choice</u> who makes them for you, truly.

III

Epilog

Question—Why didn't I write a book for black men? This is the absolute truth.

Women want to avoid reading about them and want to learn less about themselves and more about men-selves. Men follow the trend of a woman's behavior because black men chase and black women run, fall and fake injury so that black men feel that they're needed (Deception).

(Hint: Why relationships do not last because the premise is a farce)

Women want answers given to them so that they do not have to spend time on workable answers individualized to them based on their unique mind print. Women love a product that bashes men because it continues the cycle of denial.

Women:

- Raise men who do not respect women.

- Have babies with men who cannot raise men and need to finish raising themselves.

- Force an insurmountable situation with a man.

- Allow a dick to guide her relationship.

- Spend more time asking the girlfriend who wants her man, about her man, when her friend plots to take her man.

- Think being alone means not having sex.

Men do one thing that tips the scale in their favor; they manipulate a woman's need to be accepted and their fear of being alone. Men feed off women who are over weight not physically but emotionally. Men in essence are motivated by dangerous possibilities while in a malaise of sexual energy. "The Three P's", pussy, passion and personality are what women need to maintain men, not her purse, pride and procrastination.

The Three P.'s

1. Pussy-the ability to package a superior sexual experience consistently with the act itself being a didactic dessert, not the main entrée.

2. Passion-the ability to find out the desires and passions of others and express in those desires and dreams more enthusiasm and fervor than the person whose dreams they actually belong to.

3. Personality-the ability to be imaginative and free from conventional ideologies. Exuding energetic spirit abandon from judgement, expectation and presumptions.

Men do not need a manual. They need a woman with some courage and specific points about what she wants and how to get it without the deception of appeasement. You control the dynamic whether you like it or not, period! If he runs off or you think you scared him away-fuck'em. He is insufficient to know your truth and can not deal with you as a person, individual and woman. A man does what he always does, get over on his mother and think he can manipulate the heartstrings of any woman like he did and possibly still does his mother. Remember people hate to be wrong and how could daddy's little princess be wrong. It is exciting to test the limits and see how far a man can go. STOP YOUR DUMB SHIT AND CHECK HIS ASS IMMEDIATELY AT THE GATE before you end up with an empty vessel where "YOU" used to be.

The problem is Choice.

How to Save Your Time

Time is unsalvageable and can not be stored, conserved or capsulated. There is no device that can safeguard, defend or protect time. The only thing that matters when it comes down to making prudent decisions about efficient time management is your response and your decision-making ability within that moment. The number one conundrum is when you have things to do there is never enough time and when there is nothing to do you have plenty of it.

Here are some helpful ideas:

- Always assume you have something to do. This allows you the latitude to not get boxed in to a commitment you can not fulfill.

- Do not let guilt guide your decision. Enough said.

- Do not let what someone else did for you in the past control your decision. What was done for you should have been done out of kindness not expectation.

- Know how much disposable time you have in your schedule. Budget your time like you budget for your vices.

- Set limits and know when to say when. Setting limits and knowing were your cut off point is helps you avoid lying for no reason and other MENTAL dis-eases.

- If you think someone is wasting your time-they are-bounce (remove yourself from there presence) immediately. You have great gifts trust your instincts.

- Do not engage in one of our favorite past times, The Mind Game. Because the more time you make him or her invests is the same amount of time you invest. And in the end sex and emotion misdirected equal poor time management.

How to Save Your Money

Money unlike time is recoupable but nevertheless it is equally as important. Taking an unforeseen loss is understandable, but taking an unnecessary loss unforgivable. Spending money should be seemed as an act in a profitable return. Money provides you with the means to sustain or acquire personal wants and universal needs. When you spend money to attract or to convince or even persuade, you need to set boundaries to protect you from you, period.

Here are some helpful ideas:

- Do not over extend yourself to impress. Façade fades and passes. But credit cards must be paid.

- Do not buy tickets in advance. I should not have to explain this one.

- Know what is in your pocket. Check your account and do not barrow from Paul to pay the tab.

- Learn the art of simplicity. That is a place where you and your companion will be best.

List four things that you keep wasting money on.

1. _____

2. _____

3. _____

4. _____

   Now, list the real reason you repeatedly spend money on those things over and over again. _____

To the novice who thinks that negating the spending of money is the key, think again. People in general despise a miser. Selfishness is next to loneliness, which is next to a bottle of Chardonnay watching "Waiting to Exhale" trying to explain his "Disappearing Act". Saving money does not necessarily mean not spending money but first building your commonsense bank and investing wisely.

Become a conscious spender and don't let your habits and impulses rule your logic and call it love. You can not splurge spend and buy acceptance. Save your money by first saving yourself from expectations of what is "SUPPOSE TO" bring satisfaction and stability.

How to Save Your Energy

Conservationist will preach the gospel of alternative energy sources and limiting his addiction petroleum products. Solar power is too complicated an issue to be discussed although there is plenty of it. Coal is an alternative fueling source that is secretly talked about by "Anti-Americans" whom are called communist and proletariat socialist pragmatics. What is energy? Energy has been defined as: having the capacity for working: vigor.2.Strength: force.3.Vitality of expression. Let us deal with a cross of etymological practicalities and euphemistic objectivity.

E-Motion

Energy in motion that is given off in any and all directions without focus is excessive and wasteful. Only with focus and deliberate concentration can you conserve your energy. Gluttony—excess, Anger-fear paranoid rampant feelings of loss, want and the old, "never again" drive the emotional body philosophy, Lust-comfort, pleasures and desires. These great bodies of work waste more energy when they are not guided with the proper focus than anything. They are shunned away from because human beings have the biggest problem with them, ergo emotions. The body spends one-fourth of its energy digesting food and the rest organizing our mental overload of the world. In dealing with men, how much energy do you denote to avoiding them or once you have one, obsessing over them? Regardless of the fact you constantly take away from you utilizing the rest of your energy on the real problem, avoidance of any form of confrontation.

List three problems that you hate dealing with when you commit to someone (friend or Hoe):

1. _____
2. _____
3. _____

List one alternative way of saving energy to handle the three listed above.

1. _____

Helpful hints to saving your energy:

- Know when your mind tank is on low.

- Get to know your triggers and write them down.

- (When someone makes demands on you and your body lets you know what those triggers are-pay attention to those specific emotional triggers that allow you to waste energy unnecessarily.) There are a grouping of words, thoughts that create an uncomfortable feeling in you, make note of them.

- Stop worrying about men you can not control.

- One alternative energy source is your network. Do not be afraid to ask for help.

- Carry wise people in your circumference not reactionary people that like watching drama.

- Murder the guilt that comes with saying NO.

- Get your PIMP HAND strong.

- Learn that perpetuating the excuse that, "women are E-motional beings", will get you used, locked up or physically hurt.

- Master the art of less is more. Simplicity has the most dramatic affect because it is not as present in these days and times but it has the most powerful affect. (Ms. PAC-MAN Vs. Halo)

Grand acts and expensive gestures take a lot of energy to prepare, but there overall affect pales in comparison to measures and means that where thought out with simplicity and detail. The best way to save energy is to allow someone else to do the work for you and not reacting to the slightest thing said or insinuated. Allow the inertia from a man's force and action to do the work and counter his actions with a calm motion. Emotional women who are reactionary and not logical when necessary are the easiest to manipulate. T hey burn all of their energy on wasted emotions and exhausting actions and make the perfect victim.

<u>THE PROBLEM IS CHOICE!</u>

References

Tartar, Maria. The Hard Facts of the Grimm's Fairytales. Princeton, NJ: Princeton University Press, © 1987

Kast, Verena & Whitcher, Douglas. Through Emotions to Maturity: Psychological Reading of Fairytales. Fromm International Publishing Corporation ©1993

Cashdan, Sheldon. Witch Must Die: The Hidden Meaning of Fairy Tales. Basic Books, © 2000

Pittman, Frank. "Beyond Betrayal: Life After infidelity, Psychology Today: May-Jun ©1993

Smith, Robin. Lies at the Altar: The Truth about Great Marriages. Hyperion Publication, New York, New York, © 2006

Marston, Ralph. www.dailymotivators.com "Changing the Past". October 7, 2005

McCoy, Dorothy. Manipulative Man Identity Behavior: Counter the Abuse: Regain Control. Avon, Massachusetts: Adam Media, © 2006

Kimes, Joanne. Dating Sucks: What to Do when Your Love Life Makes You Miserable. Avon Massachusetts: Adam Media, © 2005

Greene, Robert. The 48 Laws of Power. New York, New York: Penguin Books, © 1998

978-0-595-49865-9
0-595-49865-5

www.ingramcontent.com/pod-product-compliance
Lightning Source LLC
Chambersburg PA
CBHW020341290526
45785CB00005B/2119